JOB APPLICATION TRACKER

DEDICATION

This Job Application Tracker is dedicated to all the people out there who want to keep their job application notes organized and document their findings in the process.

You are my inspiration for producing books and I'm honored to be a part of keeping all of your job application notes and records organized.

This journal notebook will help you record the details of which places of employment that you have applied to.

Thoughtfully put together with these sections to record: Company, Position, Found On, Agency, Direct, Salary, Applied On, Location, Commute Time & Notes.

HOW TO USE THIS BOOK

The purpose of this book is to keep all of your Job Application notes all in one place. It will help keep you organized.

This Job Application Tracker will allow you to accurately document details about places you've put your application in.

Here are examples of the prompts for you to fill in and write about your experience in this book:

1. Company - Write the name of the company, contact, their position, phone, email and notes.

2. Position - Record the position you are applying for.

3. Found On - Log where you found the opportunity.

4. Agency - Did you go through an agency or recruiter?

5. Direct - Did you find them directly yourself?

6. Salary - Write the salary they offer.

7. Applied On - Record the date you put in your application.

8. Location - Log the location.

9. Commute Time - Write the commute time for you.

10. Notes - Blank lined space for writing any additional important information you want such as whether you had an interview, how it went, how long your unemployment has been, how long you've been looking for a job, interviews coming up, etc.

JOB APPLICATION TRACKER

COMPANY		POSITION			APPLIED ON	
CONTACT		FOUND ON			LOCATION	
POSITION		AGENCY	YES	NO	ADDRESS	
PHONE		DIRECT	YES	NO		
EMAIL		SALARY			COMUTE TIME	
NOTES						

COMPANY		POSITION			APPLIED ON	
CONTACT		FOUND ON			LOCATION	
POSITION		AGENCY	YES	NO	ADDRESS	
PHONE		DIRECT	YES	NO		
EMAIL		SALARY			COMUTE TIME	
NOTES						

COMPANY		POSITION			APPLIED ON	
CONTACT		FOUND ON			LOCATION	
POSITION		AGENCY	YES	NO	ADDRESS	
PHONE		DIRECT	YES	NO		
EMAIL		SALARY			COMUTE TIME	
NOTES						

COMPANY		POSITION			APPLIED ON	
CONTACT		FOUND ON			LOCATION	
POSITION		AGENCY	YES	NO	ADDRESS	
PHONE		DIRECT	YES	NO		
EMAIL		SALARY			COMUTE TIME	
NOTES						

COMPANY		POSITION			APPLIED ON	
CONTACT		FOUND ON			LOCATION	
POSITION		AGENCY	YES	NO	ADDRESS	
PHONE		DIRECT	YES	NO		
EMAIL		SALARY			COMUTE TIME	
NOTES						

NOTES

JOB APPLICATION TRACKER

COMPANY		POSITION		APPLIED ON	
CONTACT		FOUND ON		LOCATION	
POSITION		AGENCY	YES NO	ADDRESS	
PHONE		DIRECT	YES NO		
EMAIL		SALARY		COMUTE TIME	
NOTES					

COMPANY		POSITION		APPLIED ON	
CONTACT		FOUND ON		LOCATION	
POSITION		AGENCY	YES NO	ADDRESS	
PHONE		DIRECT	YES NO		
EMAIL		SALARY		COMUTE TIME	
NOTES					

COMPANY		POSITION		APPLIED ON	
CONTACT		FOUND ON		LOCATION	
POSITION		AGENCY	YES NO	ADDRESS	
PHONE		DIRECT	YES NO		
EMAIL		SALARY		COMUTE TIME	
NOTES					

COMPANY		POSITION		APPLIED ON	
CONTACT		FOUND ON		LOCATION	
POSITION		AGENCY	YES NO	ADDRESS	
PHONE		DIRECT	YES NO		
EMAIL		SALARY		COMUTE TIME	
NOTES					

COMPANY		POSITION		APPLIED ON	
CONTACT		FOUND ON		LOCATION	
POSITION		AGENCY	YES NO	ADDRESS	
PHONE		DIRECT	YES NO		
EMAIL		SALARY		COMUTE TIME	
NOTES					

NOTES

JOB APPLICATION TRACKER

COMPANY		POSITION		APPLIED ON	
CONTACT		FOUND ON		LOCATION	
POSITION		AGENCY	YES NO	ADDRESS	
PHONE		DIRECT	YES NO		
EMAIL		SALARY		COMUTE TIME	
NOTES					

COMPANY		POSITION		APPLIED ON	
CONTACT		FOUND ON		LOCATION	
POSITION		AGENCY	YES NO	ADDRESS	
PHONE		DIRECT	YES NO		
EMAIL		SALARY		COMUTE TIME	
NOTES					

COMPANY		POSITION		APPLIED ON	
CONTACT		FOUND ON		LOCATION	
POSITION		AGENCY	YES NO	ADDRESS	
PHONE		DIRECT	YES NO		
EMAIL		SALARY		COMUTE TIME	
NOTES					

COMPANY		POSITION		APPLIED ON	
CONTACT		FOUND ON		LOCATION	
POSITION		AGENCY	YES NO	ADDRESS	
PHONE		DIRECT	YES NO		
EMAIL		SALARY		COMUTE TIME	
NOTES					

COMPANY		POSITION		APPLIED ON	
CONTACT		FOUND ON		LOCATION	
POSITION		AGENCY	YES NO	ADDRESS	
PHONE		DIRECT	YES NO		
EMAIL		SALARY		COMUTE TIME	
NOTES					

NOTES

JOB APPLICATION TRACKER

COMPANY		POSITION		APPLIED ON	
CONTACT		FOUND ON		LOCATION	
POSITION		AGENCY	YES NO	ADDRESS	
PHONE		DIRECT	YES NO		
EMAIL		SALARY		COMUTE TIME	
NOTES					

COMPANY		POSITION		APPLIED ON	
CONTACT		FOUND ON		LOCATION	
POSITION		AGENCY	YES NO	ADDRESS	
PHONE		DIRECT	YES NO		
EMAIL		SALARY		COMUTE TIME	
NOTES					

COMPANY		POSITION		APPLIED ON	
CONTACT		FOUND ON		LOCATION	
POSITION		AGENCY	YES NO	ADDRESS	
PHONE		DIRECT	YES NO		
EMAIL		SALARY		COMUTE TIME	
NOTES					

COMPANY		POSITION		APPLIED ON	
CONTACT		FOUND ON		LOCATION	
POSITION		AGENCY	YES NO	ADDRESS	
PHONE		DIRECT	YES NO		
EMAIL		SALARY		COMUTE TIME	
NOTES					

COMPANY		POSITION		APPLIED ON	
CONTACT		FOUND ON		LOCATION	
POSITION		AGENCY	YES NO	ADDRESS	
PHONE		DIRECT	YES NO		
EMAIL		SALARY		COMUTE TIME	
NOTES					

NOTES

JOB APPLICATION TRACKER

COMPANY		POSITION		APPLIED ON	
CONTACT		FOUND ON		LOCATION	
POSITION		AGENCY	YES NO	ADDRESS	
PHONE		DIRECT	YES NO		
EMAIL		SALARY		COMUTE TIME	
NOTES					

COMPANY		POSITION		APPLIED ON	
CONTACT		FOUND ON		LOCATION	
POSITION		AGENCY	YES NO	ADDRESS	
PHONE		DIRECT	YES NO		
EMAIL		SALARY		COMUTE TIME	
NOTES					

COMPANY		POSITION		APPLIED ON	
CONTACT		FOUND ON		LOCATION	
POSITION		AGENCY	YES NO	ADDRESS	
PHONE		DIRECT	YES NO		
EMAIL		SALARY		COMUTE TIME	
NOTES					

COMPANY		POSITION		APPLIED ON	
CONTACT		FOUND ON		LOCATION	
POSITION		AGENCY	YES NO	ADDRESS	
PHONE		DIRECT	YES NO		
EMAIL		SALARY		COMUTE TIME	
NOTES					

COMPANY		POSITION		APPLIED ON	
CONTACT		FOUND ON		LOCATION	
POSITION		AGENCY	YES NO	ADDRESS	
PHONE		DIRECT	YES NO		
EMAIL		SALARY		COMUTE TIME	
NOTES					

NOTES

JOB APPLICATION TRACKER

COMPANY		POSITION		APPLIED ON	
CONTACT		FOUND ON		LOCATION	
POSITION		AGENCY	YES NO	ADDRESS	
PHONE		DIRECT	YES NO		
EMAIL		SALARY		COMUTE TIME	
NOTES					

COMPANY		POSITION		APPLIED ON	
CONTACT		FOUND ON		LOCATION	
POSITION		AGENCY	YES NO	ADDRESS	
PHONE		DIRECT	YES NO		
EMAIL		SALARY		COMUTE TIME	
NOTES					

COMPANY		POSITION		APPLIED ON	
CONTACT		FOUND ON		LOCATION	
POSITION		AGENCY	YES NO	ADDRESS	
PHONE		DIRECT	YES NO		
EMAIL		SALARY		COMUTE TIME	
NOTES					

COMPANY		POSITION		APPLIED ON	
CONTACT		FOUND ON		LOCATION	
POSITION		AGENCY	YES NO	ADDRESS	
PHONE		DIRECT	YES NO		
EMAIL		SALARY		COMUTE TIME	
NOTES					

COMPANY		POSITION		APPLIED ON	
CONTACT		FOUND ON		LOCATION	
POSITION		AGENCY	YES NO	ADDRESS	
PHONE		DIRECT	YES NO		
EMAIL		SALARY		COMUTE TIME	
NOTES					

NOTES

JOB APPLICATION TRACKER

COMPANY		POSITION		APPLIED ON	
CONTACT		FOUND ON		LOCATION	
POSITION		AGENCY	YES NO	ADDRESS	
PHONE		DIRECT	YES NO		
EMAIL		SALARY		COMUTE TIME	
NOTES					

COMPANY		POSITION		APPLIED ON	
CONTACT		FOUND ON		LOCATION	
POSITION		AGENCY	YES NO	ADDRESS	
PHONE		DIRECT	YES NO		
EMAIL		SALARY		COMUTE TIME	
NOTES					

COMPANY		POSITION		APPLIED ON	
CONTACT		FOUND ON		LOCATION	
POSITION		AGENCY	YES NO	ADDRESS	
PHONE		DIRECT	YES NO		
EMAIL		SALARY		COMUTE TIME	
NOTES					

COMPANY		POSITION		APPLIED ON	
CONTACT		FOUND ON		LOCATION	
POSITION		AGENCY	YES NO	ADDRESS	
PHONE		DIRECT	YES NO		
EMAIL		SALARY		COMUTE TIME	
NOTES					

COMPANY		POSITION		APPLIED ON	
CONTACT		FOUND ON		LOCATION	
POSITION		AGENCY	YES NO	ADDRESS	
PHONE		DIRECT	YES NO		
EMAIL		SALARY		COMUTE TIME	
NOTES					

NOTES

JOB APPLICATION TRACKER

COMPANY		POSITION		APPLIED ON	
CONTACT		FOUND ON		LOCATION	
POSITION		AGENCY	YES NO	ADDRESS	
PHONE		DIRECT	YES NO		
EMAIL		SALARY		COMUTE TIME	
NOTES					

COMPANY		POSITION		APPLIED ON	
CONTACT		FOUND ON		LOCATION	
POSITION		AGENCY	YES NO	ADDRESS	
PHONE		DIRECT	YES NO		
EMAIL		SALARY		COMUTE TIME	
NOTES					

COMPANY		POSITION		APPLIED ON	
CONTACT		FOUND ON		LOCATION	
POSITION		AGENCY	YES NO	ADDRESS	
PHONE		DIRECT	YES NO		
EMAIL		SALARY		COMUTE TIME	
NOTES					

COMPANY		POSITION		APPLIED ON	
CONTACT		FOUND ON		LOCATION	
POSITION		AGENCY	YES NO	ADDRESS	
PHONE		DIRECT	YES NO		
EMAIL		SALARY		COMUTE TIME	
NOTES					

COMPANY		POSITION		APPLIED ON	
CONTACT		FOUND ON		LOCATION	
POSITION		AGENCY	YES NO	ADDRESS	
PHONE		DIRECT	YES NO		
EMAIL		SALARY		COMUTE TIME	
NOTES					

NOTES

JOB APPLICATION TRACKER

COMPANY		POSITION		APPLIED ON	
CONTACT		FOUND ON		LOCATION	
POSITION		AGENCY	YES NO	ADDRESS	
PHONE		DIRECT	YES NO		
EMAIL		SALARY		COMUTE TIME	
NOTES					

COMPANY		POSITION		APPLIED ON	
CONTACT		FOUND ON		LOCATION	
POSITION		AGENCY	YES NO	ADDRESS	
PHONE		DIRECT	YES NO		
EMAIL		SALARY		COMUTE TIME	
NOTES					

COMPANY		POSITION		APPLIED ON	
CONTACT		FOUND ON		LOCATION	
POSITION		AGENCY	YES NO	ADDRESS	
PHONE		DIRECT	YES NO		
EMAIL		SALARY		COMUTE TIME	
NOTES					

COMPANY		POSITION		APPLIED ON	
CONTACT		FOUND ON		LOCATION	
POSITION		AGENCY	YES NO	ADDRESS	
PHONE		DIRECT	YES NO		
EMAIL		SALARY		COMUTE TIME	
NOTES					

COMPANY		POSITION		APPLIED ON	
CONTACT		FOUND ON		LOCATION	
POSITION		AGENCY	YES NO	ADDRESS	
PHONE		DIRECT	YES NO		
EMAIL		SALARY		COMUTE TIME	
NOTES					

NOTES

JOB APPLICATION TRACKER

COMPANY		POSITION		APPLIED ON	
CONTACT		FOUND ON		LOCATION	
POSITION		AGENCY	YES NO	ADDRESS	
PHONE		DIRECT	YES NO		
EMAIL		SALARY		COMUTE TIME	
NOTES					

COMPANY		POSITION		APPLIED ON	
CONTACT		FOUND ON		LOCATION	
POSITION		AGENCY	YES NO	ADDRESS	
PHONE		DIRECT	YES NO		
EMAIL		SALARY		COMUTE TIME	
NOTES					

COMPANY		POSITION		APPLIED ON	
CONTACT		FOUND ON		LOCATION	
POSITION		AGENCY	YES NO	ADDRESS	
PHONE		DIRECT	YES NO		
EMAIL		SALARY		COMUTE TIME	
NOTES					

COMPANY		POSITION		APPLIED ON	
CONTACT		FOUND ON		LOCATION	
POSITION		AGENCY	YES NO	ADDRESS	
PHONE		DIRECT	YES NO		
EMAIL		SALARY		COMUTE TIME	
NOTES					

COMPANY		POSITION		APPLIED ON	
CONTACT		FOUND ON		LOCATION	
POSITION		AGENCY	YES NO	ADDRESS	
PHONE		DIRECT	YES NO		
EMAIL		SALARY		COMUTE TIME	
NOTES					

NOTES

JOB APPLICATION TRACKER

COMPANY		POSITION		APPLIED ON	
CONTACT		FOUND ON		LOCATION	
POSITION		AGENCY	YES NO	ADDRESS	
PHONE		DIRECT	YES NO		
EMAIL		SALARY		COMUTE TIME	
NOTES					

COMPANY		POSITION		APPLIED ON	
CONTACT		FOUND ON		LOCATION	
POSITION		AGENCY	YES NO	ADDRESS	
PHONE		DIRECT	YES NO		
EMAIL		SALARY		COMUTE TIME	
NOTES					

COMPANY		POSITION		APPLIED ON	
CONTACT		FOUND ON		LOCATION	
POSITION		AGENCY	YES NO	ADDRESS	
PHONE		DIRECT	YES NO		
EMAIL		SALARY		COMUTE TIME	
NOTES					

COMPANY		POSITION		APPLIED ON	
CONTACT		FOUND ON		LOCATION	
POSITION		AGENCY	YES NO	ADDRESS	
PHONE		DIRECT	YES NO		
EMAIL		SALARY		COMUTE TIME	
NOTES					

COMPANY		POSITION		APPLIED ON	
CONTACT		FOUND ON		LOCATION	
POSITION		AGENCY	YES NO	ADDRESS	
PHONE		DIRECT	YES NO		
EMAIL		SALARY		COMUTE TIME	
NOTES					

NOTES

JOB APPLICATION TRACKER

COMPANY		POSITION		APPLIED ON	
CONTACT		FOUND ON		LOCATION	
POSITION		AGENCY	YES NO	ADDRESS	
PHONE		DIRECT	YES NO		
EMAIL		SALARY		COMUTE TIME	
NOTES					

COMPANY		POSITION		APPLIED ON	
CONTACT		FOUND ON		LOCATION	
POSITION		AGENCY	YES NO	ADDRESS	
PHONE		DIRECT	YES NO		
EMAIL		SALARY		COMUTE TIME	
NOTES					

COMPANY		POSITION		APPLIED ON	
CONTACT		FOUND ON		LOCATION	
POSITION		AGENCY	YES NO	ADDRESS	
PHONE		DIRECT	YES NO		
EMAIL		SALARY		COMUTE TIME	
NOTES					

COMPANY		POSITION		APPLIED ON	
CONTACT		FOUND ON		LOCATION	
POSITION		AGENCY	YES NO	ADDRESS	
PHONE		DIRECT	YES NO		
EMAIL		SALARY		COMUTE TIME	
NOTES					

COMPANY		POSITION		APPLIED ON	
CONTACT		FOUND ON		LOCATION	
POSITION		AGENCY	YES NO	ADDRESS	
PHONE		DIRECT	YES NO		
EMAIL		SALARY		COMUTE TIME	
NOTES					

NOTES

JOB APPLICATION TRACKER

COMPANY		POSITION		APPLIED ON	
CONTACT		FOUND ON		LOCATION	
POSITION		AGENCY	YES NO	ADDRESS	
PHONE		DIRECT	YES NO		
EMAIL		SALARY		COMUTE TIME	
NOTES					

COMPANY		POSITION		APPLIED ON	
CONTACT		FOUND ON		LOCATION	
POSITION		AGENCY	YES NO	ADDRESS	
PHONE		DIRECT	YES NO		
EMAIL		SALARY		COMUTE TIME	
NOTES					

COMPANY		POSITION		APPLIED ON	
CONTACT		FOUND ON		LOCATION	
POSITION		AGENCY	YES NO	ADDRESS	
PHONE		DIRECT	YES NO		
EMAIL		SALARY		COMUTE TIME	
NOTES					

COMPANY		POSITION		APPLIED ON	
CONTACT		FOUND ON		LOCATION	
POSITION		AGENCY	YES NO	ADDRESS	
PHONE		DIRECT	YES NO		
EMAIL		SALARY		COMUTE TIME	
NOTES					

COMPANY		POSITION		APPLIED ON	
CONTACT		FOUND ON		LOCATION	
POSITION		AGENCY	YES NO	ADDRESS	
PHONE		DIRECT	YES NO		
EMAIL		SALARY		COMUTE TIME	
NOTES					

NOTES

JOB APPLICATION TRACKER

COMPANY		POSITION		APPLIED ON	
CONTACT		FOUND ON		LOCATION	
POSITION		AGENCY	YES NO	ADDRESS	
PHONE		DIRECT	YES NO		
EMAIL		SALARY		COMUTE TIME	
NOTES					

COMPANY		POSITION		APPLIED ON	
CONTACT		FOUND ON		LOCATION	
POSITION		AGENCY	YES NO	ADDRESS	
PHONE		DIRECT	YES NO		
EMAIL		SALARY		COMUTE TIME	
NOTES					

COMPANY		POSITION		APPLIED ON	
CONTACT		FOUND ON		LOCATION	
POSITION		AGENCY	YES NO	ADDRESS	
PHONE		DIRECT	YES NO		
EMAIL		SALARY		COMUTE TIME	
NOTES					

COMPANY		POSITION		APPLIED ON	
CONTACT		FOUND ON		LOCATION	
POSITION		AGENCY	YES NO	ADDRESS	
PHONE		DIRECT	YES NO		
EMAIL		SALARY		COMUTE TIME	
NOTES					

COMPANY		POSITION		APPLIED ON	
CONTACT		FOUND ON		LOCATION	
POSITION		AGENCY	YES NO	ADDRESS	
PHONE		DIRECT	YES NO		
EMAIL		SALARY		COMUTE TIME	
NOTES					

NOTES

JOB APPLICATION TRACKER

COMPANY		POSITION		APPLIED ON	
CONTACT		FOUND ON		LOCATION	
POSITION		AGENCY	YES NO	ADDRESS	
PHONE		DIRECT	YES NO		
EMAIL		SALARY		COMUTE TIME	
NOTES					

COMPANY		POSITION		APPLIED ON	
CONTACT		FOUND ON		LOCATION	
POSITION		AGENCY	YES NO	ADDRESS	
PHONE		DIRECT	YES NO		
EMAIL		SALARY		COMUTE TIME	
NOTES					

COMPANY		POSITION		APPLIED ON	
CONTACT		FOUND ON		LOCATION	
POSITION		AGENCY	YES NO	ADDRESS	
PHONE		DIRECT	YES NO		
EMAIL		SALARY		COMUTE TIME	
NOTES					

COMPANY		POSITION		APPLIED ON	
CONTACT		FOUND ON		LOCATION	
POSITION		AGENCY	YES NO	ADDRESS	
PHONE		DIRECT	YES NO		
EMAIL		SALARY		COMUTE TIME	
NOTES					

COMPANY		POSITION		APPLIED ON	
CONTACT		FOUND ON		LOCATION	
POSITION		AGENCY	YES NO	ADDRESS	
PHONE		DIRECT	YES NO		
EMAIL		SALARY		COMUTE TIME	
NOTES					

NOTES

JOB APPLICATION TRACKER

COMPANY		POSITION		APPLIED ON	
CONTACT		FOUND ON		LOCATION	
POSITION		AGENCY	YES NO	ADDRESS	
PHONE		DIRECT	YES NO		
EMAIL		SALARY		COMUTE TIME	
NOTES					

COMPANY		POSITION		APPLIED ON	
CONTACT		FOUND ON		LOCATION	
POSITION		AGENCY	YES NO	ADDRESS	
PHONE		DIRECT	YES NO		
EMAIL		SALARY		COMUTE TIME	
NOTES					

COMPANY		POSITION		APPLIED ON	
CONTACT		FOUND ON		LOCATION	
POSITION		AGENCY	YES NO	ADDRESS	
PHONE		DIRECT	YES NO		
EMAIL		SALARY		COMUTE TIME	
NOTES					

COMPANY		POSITION		APPLIED ON	
CONTACT		FOUND ON		LOCATION	
POSITION		AGENCY	YES NO	ADDRESS	
PHONE		DIRECT	YES NO		
EMAIL		SALARY		COMUTE TIME	
NOTES					

COMPANY		POSITION		APPLIED ON	
CONTACT		FOUND ON		LOCATION	
POSITION		AGENCY	YES NO	ADDRESS	
PHONE		DIRECT	YES NO		
EMAIL		SALARY		COMUTE TIME	
NOTES					

NOTES

JOB APPLICATION TRACKER

COMPANY		POSITION			APPLIED ON	
CONTACT		FOUND ON			LOCATION	
POSITION		AGENCY	YES	NO	ADDRESS	
PHONE		DIRECT	YES	NO		
EMAIL		SALARY			COMUTE TIME	
NOTES						

COMPANY		POSITION			APPLIED ON	
CONTACT		FOUND ON			LOCATION	
POSITION		AGENCY	YES	NO	ADDRESS	
PHONE		DIRECT	YES	NO		
EMAIL		SALARY			COMUTE TIME	
NOTES						

COMPANY		POSITION			APPLIED ON	
CONTACT		FOUND ON			LOCATION	
POSITION		AGENCY	YES	NO	ADDRESS	
PHONE		DIRECT	YES	NO		
EMAIL		SALARY			COMUTE TIME	
NOTES						

COMPANY		POSITION			APPLIED ON	
CONTACT		FOUND ON			LOCATION	
POSITION		AGENCY	YES	NO	ADDRESS	
PHONE		DIRECT	YES	NO		
EMAIL		SALARY			COMUTE TIME	
NOTES						

COMPANY		POSITION			APPLIED ON	
CONTACT		FOUND ON			LOCATION	
POSITION		AGENCY	YES	NO	ADDRESS	
PHONE		DIRECT	YES	NO		
EMAIL		SALARY			COMUTE TIME	
NOTES						

NOTES

JOB APPLICATION TRACKER

COMPANY		POSITION		APPLIED ON	
CONTACT		FOUND ON		LOCATION	
POSITION		AGENCY	YES NO	ADDRESS	
PHONE		DIRECT	YES NO		
EMAIL		SALARY		COMUTE TIME	
NOTES					

COMPANY		POSITION		APPLIED ON	
CONTACT		FOUND ON		LOCATION	
POSITION		AGENCY	YES NO	ADDRESS	
PHONE		DIRECT	YES NO		
EMAIL		SALARY		COMUTE TIME	
NOTES					

COMPANY		POSITION		APPLIED ON	
CONTACT		FOUND ON		LOCATION	
POSITION		AGENCY	YES NO	ADDRESS	
PHONE		DIRECT	YES NO		
EMAIL		SALARY		COMUTE TIME	
NOTES					

COMPANY		POSITION		APPLIED ON	
CONTACT		FOUND ON		LOCATION	
POSITION		AGENCY	YES NO	ADDRESS	
PHONE		DIRECT	YES NO		
EMAIL		SALARY		COMUTE TIME	
NOTES					

COMPANY		POSITION		APPLIED ON	
CONTACT		FOUND ON		LOCATION	
POSITION		AGENCY	YES NO	ADDRESS	
PHONE		DIRECT	YES NO		
EMAIL		SALARY		COMUTE TIME	
NOTES					

NOTES

JOB APPLICATION TRACKER

COMPANY		POSITION		APPLIED ON	
CONTACT		FOUND ON		LOCATION	
POSITION		AGENCY	YES NO	ADDRESS	
PHONE		DIRECT	YES NO		
EMAIL		SALARY		COMUTE TIME	
NOTES					

COMPANY		POSITION		APPLIED ON	
CONTACT		FOUND ON		LOCATION	
POSITION		AGENCY	YES NO	ADDRESS	
PHONE		DIRECT	YES NO		
EMAIL		SALARY		COMUTE TIME	
NOTES					

COMPANY		POSITION		APPLIED ON	
CONTACT		FOUND ON		LOCATION	
POSITION		AGENCY	YES NO	ADDRESS	
PHONE		DIRECT	YES NO		
EMAIL		SALARY		COMUTE TIME	
NOTES					

COMPANY		POSITION		APPLIED ON	
CONTACT		FOUND ON		LOCATION	
POSITION		AGENCY	YES NO	ADDRESS	
PHONE		DIRECT	YES NO		
EMAIL		SALARY		COMUTE TIME	
NOTES					

COMPANY		POSITION		APPLIED ON	
CONTACT		FOUND ON		LOCATION	
POSITION		AGENCY	YES NO	ADDRESS	
PHONE		DIRECT	YES NO		
EMAIL		SALARY		COMUTE TIME	
NOTES					

NOTES

JOB APPLICATION TRACKER

COMPANY		POSITION		APPLIED ON	
CONTACT		FOUND ON		LOCATION	
POSITION		AGENCY	YES NO	ADDRESS	
PHONE		DIRECT	YES NO		
EMAIL		SALARY		COMUTE TIME	
NOTES					

COMPANY		POSITION		APPLIED ON	
CONTACT		FOUND ON		LOCATION	
POSITION		AGENCY	YES NO	ADDRESS	
PHONE		DIRECT	YES NO		
EMAIL		SALARY		COMUTE TIME	
NOTES					

COMPANY		POSITION		APPLIED ON	
CONTACT		FOUND ON		LOCATION	
POSITION		AGENCY	YES NO	ADDRESS	
PHONE		DIRECT	YES NO		
EMAIL		SALARY		COMUTE TIME	
NOTES					

COMPANY		POSITION		APPLIED ON	
CONTACT		FOUND ON		LOCATION	
POSITION		AGENCY	YES NO	ADDRESS	
PHONE		DIRECT	YES NO		
EMAIL		SALARY		COMUTE TIME	
NOTES					

COMPANY		POSITION		APPLIED ON	
CONTACT		FOUND ON		LOCATION	
POSITION		AGENCY	YES NO	ADDRESS	
PHONE		DIRECT	YES NO		
EMAIL		SALARY		COMUTE TIME	
NOTES					

NOTES

JOB APPLICATION TRACKER

COMPANY		POSITION		APPLIED ON	
CONTACT		FOUND ON		LOCATION	
POSITION		AGENCY	YES NO	ADDRESS	
PHONE		DIRECT	YES NO		
EMAIL		SALARY		COMUTE TIME	
NOTES					

COMPANY		POSITION		APPLIED ON	
CONTACT		FOUND ON		LOCATION	
POSITION		AGENCY	YES NO	ADDRESS	
PHONE		DIRECT	YES NO		
EMAIL		SALARY		COMUTE TIME	
NOTES					

COMPANY		POSITION		APPLIED ON	
CONTACT		FOUND ON		LOCATION	
POSITION		AGENCY	YES NO	ADDRESS	
PHONE		DIRECT	YES NO		
EMAIL		SALARY		COMUTE TIME	
NOTES					

COMPANY		POSITION		APPLIED ON	
CONTACT		FOUND ON		LOCATION	
POSITION		AGENCY	YES NO	ADDRESS	
PHONE		DIRECT	YES NO		
EMAIL		SALARY		COMUTE TIME	
NOTES					

COMPANY		POSITION		APPLIED ON	
CONTACT		FOUND ON		LOCATION	
POSITION		AGENCY	YES NO	ADDRESS	
PHONE		DIRECT	YES NO		
EMAIL		SALARY		COMUTE TIME	
NOTES					

NOTES

JOB APPLICATION TRACKER

COMPANY		POSITION		APPLIED ON	
CONTACT		FOUND ON		LOCATION	
POSITION		AGENCY	YES NO	ADDRESS	
PHONE		DIRECT	YES NO		
EMAIL		SALARY		COMUTE TIME	
NOTES					

COMPANY		POSITION		APPLIED ON	
CONTACT		FOUND ON		LOCATION	
POSITION		AGENCY	YES NO	ADDRESS	
PHONE		DIRECT	YES NO		
EMAIL		SALARY		COMUTE TIME	
NOTES					

COMPANY		POSITION		APPLIED ON	
CONTACT		FOUND ON		LOCATION	
POSITION		AGENCY	YES NO	ADDRESS	
PHONE		DIRECT	YES NO		
EMAIL		SALARY		COMUTE TIME	
NOTES					

COMPANY		POSITION		APPLIED ON	
CONTACT		FOUND ON		LOCATION	
POSITION		AGENCY	YES NO	ADDRESS	
PHONE		DIRECT	YES NO		
EMAIL		SALARY		COMUTE TIME	
NOTES					

COMPANY		POSITION		APPLIED ON	
CONTACT		FOUND ON		LOCATION	
POSITION		AGENCY	YES NO	ADDRESS	
PHONE		DIRECT	YES NO		
EMAIL		SALARY		COMUTE TIME	
NOTES					

NOTES

JOB APPLICATION TRACKER

COMPANY		POSITION		APPLIED ON	
CONTACT		FOUND ON		LOCATION	
POSITION		AGENCY	YES NO	ADDRESS	
PHONE		DIRECT	YES NO		
EMAIL		SALARY		COMUTE TIME	
NOTES					

COMPANY		POSITION		APPLIED ON	
CONTACT		FOUND ON		LOCATION	
POSITION		AGENCY	YES NO	ADDRESS	
PHONE		DIRECT	YES NO		
EMAIL		SALARY		COMUTE TIME	
NOTES					

COMPANY		POSITION		APPLIED ON	
CONTACT		FOUND ON		LOCATION	
POSITION		AGENCY	YES NO	ADDRESS	
PHONE		DIRECT	YES NO		
EMAIL		SALARY		COMUTE TIME	
NOTES					

COMPANY		POSITION		APPLIED ON	
CONTACT		FOUND ON		LOCATION	
POSITION		AGENCY	YES NO	ADDRESS	
PHONE		DIRECT	YES NO		
EMAIL		SALARY		COMUTE TIME	
NOTES					

COMPANY		POSITION		APPLIED ON	
CONTACT		FOUND ON		LOCATION	
POSITION		AGENCY	YES NO	ADDRESS	
PHONE		DIRECT	YES NO		
EMAIL		SALARY		COMUTE TIME	
NOTES					

NOTES

JOB APPLICATION TRACKER

COMPANY		POSITION		APPLIED ON	
CONTACT		FOUND ON		LOCATION	
POSITION		AGENCY	YES NO	ADDRESS	
PHONE		DIRECT	YES NO		
EMAIL		SALARY		COMUTE TIME	
NOTES					

COMPANY		POSITION		APPLIED ON	
CONTACT		FOUND ON		LOCATION	
POSITION		AGENCY	YES NO	ADDRESS	
PHONE		DIRECT	YES NO		
EMAIL		SALARY		COMUTE TIME	
NOTES					

COMPANY		POSITION		APPLIED ON	
CONTACT		FOUND ON		LOCATION	
POSITION		AGENCY	YES NO	ADDRESS	
PHONE		DIRECT	YES NO		
EMAIL		SALARY		COMUTE TIME	
NOTES					

COMPANY		POSITION		APPLIED ON	
CONTACT		FOUND ON		LOCATION	
POSITION		AGENCY	YES NO	ADDRESS	
PHONE		DIRECT	YES NO		
EMAIL		SALARY		COMUTE TIME	
NOTES					

COMPANY		POSITION		APPLIED ON	
CONTACT		FOUND ON		LOCATION	
POSITION		AGENCY	YES NO	ADDRESS	
PHONE		DIRECT	YES NO		
EMAIL		SALARY		COMUTE TIME	
NOTES					

NOTES

JOB APPLICATION TRACKER

COMPANY		POSITION		APPLIED ON	
CONTACT		FOUND ON		LOCATION	
POSITION		AGENCY	YES NO	ADDRESS	
PHONE		DIRECT	YES NO		
EMAIL		SALARY		COMUTE TIME	
NOTES					

COMPANY		POSITION		APPLIED ON	
CONTACT		FOUND ON		LOCATION	
POSITION		AGENCY	YES NO	ADDRESS	
PHONE		DIRECT	YES NO		
EMAIL		SALARY		COMUTE TIME	
NOTES					

COMPANY		POSITION		APPLIED ON	
CONTACT		FOUND ON		LOCATION	
POSITION		AGENCY	YES NO	ADDRESS	
PHONE		DIRECT	YES NO		
EMAIL		SALARY		COMUTE TIME	
NOTES					

COMPANY		POSITION		APPLIED ON	
CONTACT		FOUND ON		LOCATION	
POSITION		AGENCY	YES NO	ADDRESS	
PHONE		DIRECT	YES NO		
EMAIL		SALARY		COMUTE TIME	
NOTES					

COMPANY		POSITION		APPLIED ON	
CONTACT		FOUND ON		LOCATION	
POSITION		AGENCY	YES NO	ADDRESS	
PHONE		DIRECT	YES NO		
EMAIL		SALARY		COMUTE TIME	
NOTES					

NOTES

JOB APPLICATION TRACKER

COMPANY		POSITION		APPLIED ON	
CONTACT		FOUND ON		LOCATION	
POSITION		AGENCY	YES NO	ADDRESS	
PHONE		DIRECT	YES NO		
EMAIL		SALARY		COMUTE TIME	
NOTES					

COMPANY		POSITION		APPLIED ON	
CONTACT		FOUND ON		LOCATION	
POSITION		AGENCY	YES NO	ADDRESS	
PHONE		DIRECT	YES NO		
EMAIL		SALARY		COMUTE TIME	
NOTES					

COMPANY		POSITION		APPLIED ON	
CONTACT		FOUND ON		LOCATION	
POSITION		AGENCY	YES NO	ADDRESS	
PHONE		DIRECT	YES NO		
EMAIL		SALARY		COMUTE TIME	
NOTES					

COMPANY		POSITION		APPLIED ON	
CONTACT		FOUND ON		LOCATION	
POSITION		AGENCY	YES NO	ADDRESS	
PHONE		DIRECT	YES NO		
EMAIL		SALARY		COMUTE TIME	
NOTES					

COMPANY		POSITION		APPLIED ON	
CONTACT		FOUND ON		LOCATION	
POSITION		AGENCY	YES NO	ADDRESS	
PHONE		DIRECT	YES NO		
EMAIL		SALARY		COMUTE TIME	
NOTES					

NOTES

JOB APPLICATION TRACKER

COMPANY		POSITION		APPLIED ON	
CONTACT		FOUND ON		LOCATION	
POSITION		AGENCY	YES NO	ADDRESS	
PHONE		DIRECT	YES NO		
EMAIL		SALARY		COMUTE TIME	
NOTES					

COMPANY		POSITION		APPLIED ON	
CONTACT		FOUND ON		LOCATION	
POSITION		AGENCY	YES NO	ADDRESS	
PHONE		DIRECT	YES NO		
EMAIL		SALARY		COMUTE TIME	
NOTES					

COMPANY		POSITION		APPLIED ON	
CONTACT		FOUND ON		LOCATION	
POSITION		AGENCY	YES NO	ADDRESS	
PHONE		DIRECT	YES NO		
EMAIL		SALARY		COMUTE TIME	
NOTES					

COMPANY		POSITION		APPLIED ON	
CONTACT		FOUND ON		LOCATION	
POSITION		AGENCY	YES NO	ADDRESS	
PHONE		DIRECT	YES NO		
EMAIL		SALARY		COMUTE TIME	
NOTES					

COMPANY		POSITION		APPLIED ON	
CONTACT		FOUND ON		LOCATION	
POSITION		AGENCY	YES NO	ADDRESS	
PHONE		DIRECT	YES NO		
EMAIL		SALARY		COMUTE TIME	
NOTES					

NOTES

JOB APPLICATION TRACKER

COMPANY		POSITION		APPLIED ON	
CONTACT		FOUND ON		LOCATION	
POSITION		AGENCY	YES NO	ADDRESS	
PHONE		DIRECT	YES NO		
EMAIL		SALARY		COMUTE TIME	
NOTES					

COMPANY		POSITION		APPLIED ON	
CONTACT		FOUND ON		LOCATION	
POSITION		AGENCY	YES NO	ADDRESS	
PHONE		DIRECT	YES NO		
EMAIL		SALARY		COMUTE TIME	
NOTES					

COMPANY		POSITION		APPLIED ON	
CONTACT		FOUND ON		LOCATION	
POSITION		AGENCY	YES NO	ADDRESS	
PHONE		DIRECT	YES NO		
EMAIL		SALARY		COMUTE TIME	
NOTES					

COMPANY		POSITION		APPLIED ON	
CONTACT		FOUND ON		LOCATION	
POSITION		AGENCY	YES NO	ADDRESS	
PHONE		DIRECT	YES NO		
EMAIL		SALARY		COMUTE TIME	
NOTES					

COMPANY		POSITION		APPLIED ON	
CONTACT		FOUND ON		LOCATION	
POSITION		AGENCY	YES NO	ADDRESS	
PHONE		DIRECT	YES NO		
EMAIL		SALARY		COMUTE TIME	
NOTES					

NOTES

JOB APPLICATION TRACKER

COMPANY		POSITION		APPLIED ON	
CONTACT		FOUND ON		LOCATION	
POSITION		AGENCY	YES NO	ADDRESS	
PHONE		DIRECT	YES NO		
EMAIL		SALARY		COMUTE TIME	
NOTES					

COMPANY		POSITION		APPLIED ON	
CONTACT		FOUND ON		LOCATION	
POSITION		AGENCY	YES NO	ADDRESS	
PHONE		DIRECT	YES NO		
EMAIL		SALARY		COMUTE TIME	
NOTES					

COMPANY		POSITION		APPLIED ON	
CONTACT		FOUND ON		LOCATION	
POSITION		AGENCY	YES NO	ADDRESS	
PHONE		DIRECT	YES NO		
EMAIL		SALARY		COMUTE TIME	
NOTES					

COMPANY		POSITION		APPLIED ON	
CONTACT		FOUND ON		LOCATION	
POSITION		AGENCY	YES NO	ADDRESS	
PHONE		DIRECT	YES NO		
EMAIL		SALARY		COMUTE TIME	
NOTES					

COMPANY		POSITION		APPLIED ON	
CONTACT		FOUND ON		LOCATION	
POSITION		AGENCY	YES NO	ADDRESS	
PHONE		DIRECT	YES NO		
EMAIL		SALARY		COMUTE TIME	
NOTES					

NOTES

JOB APPLICATION TRACKER

COMPANY		POSITION			APPLIED ON	
CONTACT		FOUND ON			LOCATION	
POSITION		AGENCY	YES	NO	ADDRESS	
PHONE		DIRECT	YES	NO		
EMAIL		SALARY			COMUTE TIME	
NOTES						

COMPANY		POSITION			APPLIED ON	
CONTACT		FOUND ON			LOCATION	
POSITION		AGENCY	YES	NO	ADDRESS	
PHONE		DIRECT	YES	NO		
EMAIL		SALARY			COMUTE TIME	
NOTES						

COMPANY		POSITION			APPLIED ON	
CONTACT		FOUND ON			LOCATION	
POSITION		AGENCY	YES	NO	ADDRESS	
PHONE		DIRECT	YES	NO		
EMAIL		SALARY			COMUTE TIME	
NOTES						

COMPANY		POSITION			APPLIED ON	
CONTACT		FOUND ON			LOCATION	
POSITION		AGENCY	YES	NO	ADDRESS	
PHONE		DIRECT	YES	NO		
EMAIL		SALARY			COMUTE TIME	
NOTES						

COMPANY		POSITION			APPLIED ON	
CONTACT		FOUND ON			LOCATION	
POSITION		AGENCY	YES	NO	ADDRESS	
PHONE		DIRECT	YES	NO		
EMAIL		SALARY			COMUTE TIME	
NOTES						

NOTES

JOB APPLICATION TRACKER

COMPANY		POSITION		APPLIED ON	
CONTACT		FOUND ON		LOCATION	
POSITION		AGENCY	YES NO	ADDRESS	
PHONE		DIRECT	YES NO		
EMAIL		SALARY		COMUTE TIME	
NOTES					

COMPANY		POSITION		APPLIED ON	
CONTACT		FOUND ON		LOCATION	
POSITION		AGENCY	YES NO	ADDRESS	
PHONE		DIRECT	YES NO		
EMAIL		SALARY		COMUTE TIME	
NOTES					

COMPANY		POSITION		APPLIED ON	
CONTACT		FOUND ON		LOCATION	
POSITION		AGENCY	YES NO	ADDRESS	
PHONE		DIRECT	YES NO		
EMAIL		SALARY		COMUTE TIME	
NOTES					

COMPANY		POSITION		APPLIED ON	
CONTACT		FOUND ON		LOCATION	
POSITION		AGENCY	YES NO	ADDRESS	
PHONE		DIRECT	YES NO		
EMAIL		SALARY		COMUTE TIME	
NOTES					

COMPANY		POSITION		APPLIED ON	
CONTACT		FOUND ON		LOCATION	
POSITION		AGENCY	YES NO	ADDRESS	
PHONE		DIRECT	YES NO		
EMAIL		SALARY		COMUTE TIME	
NOTES					

NOTES

JOB APPLICATION TRACKER

COMPANY		POSITION		APPLIED ON	
CONTACT		FOUND ON		LOCATION	
POSITION		AGENCY	YES NO	ADDRESS	
PHONE		DIRECT	YES NO		
EMAIL		SALARY		COMUTE TIME	
NOTES					

COMPANY		POSITION		APPLIED ON	
CONTACT		FOUND ON		LOCATION	
POSITION		AGENCY	YES NO	ADDRESS	
PHONE		DIRECT	YES NO		
EMAIL		SALARY		COMUTE TIME	
NOTES					

COMPANY		POSITION		APPLIED ON	
CONTACT		FOUND ON		LOCATION	
POSITION		AGENCY	YES NO	ADDRESS	
PHONE		DIRECT	YES NO		
EMAIL		SALARY		COMUTE TIME	
NOTES					

COMPANY		POSITION		APPLIED ON	
CONTACT		FOUND ON		LOCATION	
POSITION		AGENCY	YES NO	ADDRESS	
PHONE		DIRECT	YES NO		
EMAIL		SALARY		COMUTE TIME	
NOTES					

COMPANY		POSITION		APPLIED ON	
CONTACT		FOUND ON		LOCATION	
POSITION		AGENCY	YES NO	ADDRESS	
PHONE		DIRECT	YES NO		
EMAIL		SALARY		COMUTE TIME	
NOTES					

NOTES

JOB APPLICATION TRACKER

COMPANY		POSITION		APPLIED ON	
CONTACT		FOUND ON		LOCATION	
POSITION		AGENCY	YES NO	ADDRESS	
PHONE		DIRECT	YES NO		
EMAIL		SALARY		COMUTE TIME	
NOTES					

COMPANY		POSITION		APPLIED ON	
CONTACT		FOUND ON		LOCATION	
POSITION		AGENCY	YES NO	ADDRESS	
PHONE		DIRECT	YES NO		
EMAIL		SALARY		COMUTE TIME	
NOTES					

COMPANY		POSITION		APPLIED ON	
CONTACT		FOUND ON		LOCATION	
POSITION		AGENCY	YES NO	ADDRESS	
PHONE		DIRECT	YES NO		
EMAIL		SALARY		COMUTE TIME	
NOTES					

COMPANY		POSITION		APPLIED ON	
CONTACT		FOUND ON		LOCATION	
POSITION		AGENCY	YES NO	ADDRESS	
PHONE		DIRECT	YES NO		
EMAIL		SALARY		COMUTE TIME	
NOTES					

COMPANY		POSITION		APPLIED ON	
CONTACT		FOUND ON		LOCATION	
POSITION		AGENCY	YES NO	ADDRESS	
PHONE		DIRECT	YES NO		
EMAIL		SALARY		COMUTE TIME	
NOTES					

NOTES

JOB APPLICATION TRACKER

COMPANY		POSITION		APPLIED ON	
CONTACT		FOUND ON		LOCATION	
POSITION		AGENCY	YES NO	ADDRESS	
PHONE		DIRECT	YES NO		
EMAIL		SALARY		COMUTE TIME	
NOTES					

COMPANY		POSITION		APPLIED ON	
CONTACT		FOUND ON		LOCATION	
POSITION		AGENCY	YES NO	ADDRESS	
PHONE		DIRECT	YES NO		
EMAIL		SALARY		COMUTE TIME	
NOTES					

COMPANY		POSITION		APPLIED ON	
CONTACT		FOUND ON		LOCATION	
POSITION		AGENCY	YES NO	ADDRESS	
PHONE		DIRECT	YES NO		
EMAIL		SALARY		COMUTE TIME	
NOTES					

COMPANY		POSITION		APPLIED ON	
CONTACT		FOUND ON		LOCATION	
POSITION		AGENCY	YES NO	ADDRESS	
PHONE		DIRECT	YES NO		
EMAIL		SALARY		COMUTE TIME	
NOTES					

COMPANY		POSITION		APPLIED ON	
CONTACT		FOUND ON		LOCATION	
POSITION		AGENCY	YES NO	ADDRESS	
PHONE		DIRECT	YES NO		
EMAIL		SALARY		COMUTE TIME	
NOTES					

NOTES

JOB APPLICATION TRACKER

COMPANY		POSITION		APPLIED ON	
CONTACT		FOUND ON		LOCATION	
POSITION		AGENCY	YES NO	ADDRESS	
PHONE		DIRECT	YES NO		
EMAIL		SALARY		COMUTE TIME	
NOTES					

COMPANY		POSITION		APPLIED ON	
CONTACT		FOUND ON		LOCATION	
POSITION		AGENCY	YES NO	ADDRESS	
PHONE		DIRECT	YES NO		
EMAIL		SALARY		COMUTE TIME	
NOTES					

COMPANY		POSITION		APPLIED ON	
CONTACT		FOUND ON		LOCATION	
POSITION		AGENCY	YES NO	ADDRESS	
PHONE		DIRECT	YES NO		
EMAIL		SALARY		COMUTE TIME	
NOTES					

COMPANY		POSITION		APPLIED ON	
CONTACT		FOUND ON		LOCATION	
POSITION		AGENCY	YES NO	ADDRESS	
PHONE		DIRECT	YES NO		
EMAIL		SALARY		COMUTE TIME	
NOTES					

COMPANY		POSITION		APPLIED ON	
CONTACT		FOUND ON		LOCATION	
POSITION		AGENCY	YES NO	ADDRESS	
PHONE		DIRECT	YES NO		
EMAIL		SALARY		COMUTE TIME	
NOTES					

NOTES

JOB APPLICATION TRACKER

COMPANY		POSITION		APPLIED ON	
CONTACT		FOUND ON		LOCATION	
POSITION		AGENCY	YES NO	ADDRESS	
PHONE		DIRECT	YES NO		
EMAIL		SALARY		COMUTE TIME	
NOTES					

COMPANY		POSITION		APPLIED ON	
CONTACT		FOUND ON		LOCATION	
POSITION		AGENCY	YES NO	ADDRESS	
PHONE		DIRECT	YES NO		
EMAIL		SALARY		COMUTE TIME	
NOTES					

COMPANY		POSITION		APPLIED ON	
CONTACT		FOUND ON		LOCATION	
POSITION		AGENCY	YES NO	ADDRESS	
PHONE		DIRECT	YES NO		
EMAIL		SALARY		COMUTE TIME	
NOTES					

COMPANY		POSITION		APPLIED ON	
CONTACT		FOUND ON		LOCATION	
POSITION		AGENCY	YES NO	ADDRESS	
PHONE		DIRECT	YES NO		
EMAIL		SALARY		COMUTE TIME	
NOTES					

COMPANY		POSITION		APPLIED ON	
CONTACT		FOUND ON		LOCATION	
POSITION		AGENCY	YES NO	ADDRESS	
PHONE		DIRECT	YES NO		
EMAIL		SALARY		COMUTE TIME	
NOTES					

NOTES

JOB APPLICATION TRACKER

COMPANY		POSITION		APPLIED ON	
CONTACT		FOUND ON		LOCATION	
POSITION		AGENCY	YES NO	ADDRESS	
PHONE		DIRECT	YES NO		
EMAIL		SALARY		COMUTE TIME	
NOTES					

COMPANY		POSITION		APPLIED ON	
CONTACT		FOUND ON		LOCATION	
POSITION		AGENCY	YES NO	ADDRESS	
PHONE		DIRECT	YES NO		
EMAIL		SALARY		COMUTE TIME	
NOTES					

COMPANY		POSITION		APPLIED ON	
CONTACT		FOUND ON		LOCATION	
POSITION		AGENCY	YES NO	ADDRESS	
PHONE		DIRECT	YES NO		
EMAIL		SALARY		COMUTE TIME	
NOTES					

COMPANY		POSITION		APPLIED ON	
CONTACT		FOUND ON		LOCATION	
POSITION		AGENCY	YES NO	ADDRESS	
PHONE		DIRECT	YES NO		
EMAIL		SALARY		COMUTE TIME	
NOTES					

COMPANY		POSITION		APPLIED ON	
CONTACT		FOUND ON		LOCATION	
POSITION		AGENCY	YES NO	ADDRESS	
PHONE		DIRECT	YES NO		
EMAIL		SALARY		COMUTE TIME	
NOTES					

NOTES

JOB APPLICATION TRACKER

COMPANY		POSITION		APPLIED ON	
CONTACT		FOUND ON		LOCATION	
POSITION		AGENCY	YES NO	ADDRESS	
PHONE		DIRECT	YES NO		
EMAIL		SALARY		COMUTE TIME	
NOTES					

COMPANY		POSITION		APPLIED ON	
CONTACT		FOUND ON		LOCATION	
POSITION		AGENCY	YES NO	ADDRESS	
PHONE		DIRECT	YES NO		
EMAIL		SALARY		COMUTE TIME	
NOTES					

COMPANY		POSITION		APPLIED ON	
CONTACT		FOUND ON		LOCATION	
POSITION		AGENCY	YES NO	ADDRESS	
PHONE		DIRECT	YES NO		
EMAIL		SALARY		COMUTE TIME	
NOTES					

COMPANY		POSITION		APPLIED ON	
CONTACT		FOUND ON		LOCATION	
POSITION		AGENCY	YES NO	ADDRESS	
PHONE		DIRECT	YES NO		
EMAIL		SALARY		COMUTE TIME	
NOTES					

COMPANY		POSITION		APPLIED ON	
CONTACT		FOUND ON		LOCATION	
POSITION		AGENCY	YES NO	ADDRESS	
PHONE		DIRECT	YES NO		
EMAIL		SALARY		COMUTE TIME	
NOTES					

NOTES

JOB APPLICATION TRACKER

COMPANY		POSITION		APPLIED ON	
CONTACT		FOUND ON		LOCATION	
POSITION		AGENCY	YES NO	ADDRESS	
PHONE		DIRECT	YES NO		
EMAIL		SALARY		COMUTE TIME	
NOTES					

COMPANY		POSITION		APPLIED ON	
CONTACT		FOUND ON		LOCATION	
POSITION		AGENCY	YES NO	ADDRESS	
PHONE		DIRECT	YES NO		
EMAIL		SALARY		COMUTE TIME	
NOTES					

COMPANY		POSITION		APPLIED ON	
CONTACT		FOUND ON		LOCATION	
POSITION		AGENCY	YES NO	ADDRESS	
PHONE		DIRECT	YES NO		
EMAIL		SALARY		COMUTE TIME	
NOTES					

COMPANY		POSITION		APPLIED ON	
CONTACT		FOUND ON		LOCATION	
POSITION		AGENCY	YES NO	ADDRESS	
PHONE		DIRECT	YES NO		
EMAIL		SALARY		COMUTE TIME	
NOTES					

COMPANY		POSITION		APPLIED ON	
CONTACT		FOUND ON		LOCATION	
POSITION		AGENCY	YES NO	ADDRESS	
PHONE		DIRECT	YES NO		
EMAIL		SALARY		COMUTE TIME	
NOTES					

NOTES

JOB APPLICATION TRACKER

COMPANY		POSITION		APPLIED ON	
CONTACT		FOUND ON		LOCATION	
POSITION		AGENCY	YES NO	ADDRESS	
PHONE		DIRECT	YES NO		
EMAIL		SALARY		COMUTE TIME	
NOTES					

COMPANY		POSITION		APPLIED ON	
CONTACT		FOUND ON		LOCATION	
POSITION		AGENCY	YES NO	ADDRESS	
PHONE		DIRECT	YES NO		
EMAIL		SALARY		COMUTE TIME	
NOTES					

COMPANY		POSITION		APPLIED ON	
CONTACT		FOUND ON		LOCATION	
POSITION		AGENCY	YES NO	ADDRESS	
PHONE		DIRECT	YES NO		
EMAIL		SALARY		COMUTE TIME	
NOTES					

COMPANY		POSITION		APPLIED ON	
CONTACT		FOUND ON		LOCATION	
POSITION		AGENCY	YES NO	ADDRESS	
PHONE		DIRECT	YES NO		
EMAIL		SALARY		COMUTE TIME	
NOTES					

COMPANY		POSITION		APPLIED ON	
CONTACT		FOUND ON		LOCATION	
POSITION		AGENCY	YES NO	ADDRESS	
PHONE		DIRECT	YES NO		
EMAIL		SALARY		COMUTE TIME	
NOTES					

NOTES

JOB APPLICATION TRACKER

COMPANY		POSITION		APPLIED ON	
CONTACT		FOUND ON		LOCATION	
POSITION		AGENCY	YES NO	ADDRESS	
PHONE		DIRECT	YES NO		
EMAIL		SALARY		COMUTE TIME	
NOTES					

COMPANY		POSITION		APPLIED ON	
CONTACT		FOUND ON		LOCATION	
POSITION		AGENCY	YES NO	ADDRESS	
PHONE		DIRECT	YES NO		
EMAIL		SALARY		COMUTE TIME	
NOTES					

COMPANY		POSITION		APPLIED ON	
CONTACT		FOUND ON		LOCATION	
POSITION		AGENCY	YES NO	ADDRESS	
PHONE		DIRECT	YES NO		
EMAIL		SALARY		COMUTE TIME	
NOTES					

COMPANY		POSITION		APPLIED ON	
CONTACT		FOUND ON		LOCATION	
POSITION		AGENCY	YES NO	ADDRESS	
PHONE		DIRECT	YES NO		
EMAIL		SALARY		COMUTE TIME	
NOTES					

COMPANY		POSITION		APPLIED ON	
CONTACT		FOUND ON		LOCATION	
POSITION		AGENCY	YES NO	ADDRESS	
PHONE		DIRECT	YES NO		
EMAIL		SALARY		COMUTE TIME	
NOTES					

NOTES

JOB APPLICATION TRACKER

COMPANY		POSITION		APPLIED ON	
CONTACT		FOUND ON		LOCATION	
POSITION		AGENCY	YES NO	ADDRESS	
PHONE		DIRECT	YES NO		
EMAIL		SALARY		COMUTE TIME	
NOTES					

COMPANY		POSITION		APPLIED ON	
CONTACT		FOUND ON		LOCATION	
POSITION		AGENCY	YES NO	ADDRESS	
PHONE		DIRECT	YES NO		
EMAIL		SALARY		COMUTE TIME	
NOTES					

COMPANY		POSITION		APPLIED ON	
CONTACT		FOUND ON		LOCATION	
POSITION		AGENCY	YES NO	ADDRESS	
PHONE		DIRECT	YES NO		
EMAIL		SALARY		COMUTE TIME	
NOTES					

COMPANY		POSITION		APPLIED ON	
CONTACT		FOUND ON		LOCATION	
POSITION		AGENCY	YES NO	ADDRESS	
PHONE		DIRECT	YES NO		
EMAIL		SALARY		COMUTE TIME	
NOTES					

COMPANY		POSITION		APPLIED ON	
CONTACT		FOUND ON		LOCATION	
POSITION		AGENCY	YES NO	ADDRESS	
PHONE		DIRECT	YES NO		
EMAIL		SALARY		COMUTE TIME	
NOTES					

NOTES

JOB APPLICATION TRACKER

COMPANY		POSITION			APPLIED ON	
CONTACT		FOUND ON			LOCATION	
POSITION		AGENCY	YES	NO	ADDRESS	
PHONE		DIRECT	YES	NO		
EMAIL		SALARY			COMUTE TIME	
NOTES						

COMPANY		POSITION			APPLIED ON	
CONTACT		FOUND ON			LOCATION	
POSITION		AGENCY	YES	NO	ADDRESS	
PHONE		DIRECT	YES	NO		
EMAIL		SALARY			COMUTE TIME	
NOTES						

COMPANY		POSITION			APPLIED ON	
CONTACT		FOUND ON			LOCATION	
POSITION		AGENCY	YES	NO	ADDRESS	
PHONE		DIRECT	YES	NO		
EMAIL		SALARY			COMUTE TIME	
NOTES						

COMPANY		POSITION			APPLIED ON	
CONTACT		FOUND ON			LOCATION	
POSITION		AGENCY	YES	NO	ADDRESS	
PHONE		DIRECT	YES	NO		
EMAIL		SALARY			COMUTE TIME	
NOTES						

COMPANY		POSITION			APPLIED ON	
CONTACT		FOUND ON			LOCATION	
POSITION		AGENCY	YES	NO	ADDRESS	
PHONE		DIRECT	YES	NO		
EMAIL		SALARY			COMUTE TIME	
NOTES						

NOTES

JOB APPLICATION TRACKER

COMPANY		POSITION		APPLIED ON	
CONTACT		FOUND ON		LOCATION	
POSITION		AGENCY	YES NO	ADDRESS	
PHONE		DIRECT	YES NO		
EMAIL		SALARY		COMUTE TIME	
NOTES					

COMPANY		POSITION		APPLIED ON	
CONTACT		FOUND ON		LOCATION	
POSITION		AGENCY	YES NO	ADDRESS	
PHONE		DIRECT	YES NO		
EMAIL		SALARY		COMUTE TIME	
NOTES					

COMPANY		POSITION		APPLIED ON	
CONTACT		FOUND ON		LOCATION	
POSITION		AGENCY	YES NO	ADDRESS	
PHONE		DIRECT	YES NO		
EMAIL		SALARY		COMUTE TIME	
NOTES					

COMPANY		POSITION		APPLIED ON	
CONTACT		FOUND ON		LOCATION	
POSITION		AGENCY	YES NO	ADDRESS	
PHONE		DIRECT	YES NO		
EMAIL		SALARY		COMUTE TIME	
NOTES					

COMPANY		POSITION		APPLIED ON	
CONTACT		FOUND ON		LOCATION	
POSITION		AGENCY	YES NO	ADDRESS	
PHONE		DIRECT	YES NO		
EMAIL		SALARY		COMUTE TIME	
NOTES					

NOTES

JOB APPLICATION TRACKER

COMPANY		POSITION			APPLIED ON	
CONTACT		FOUND ON			LOCATION	
POSITION		AGENCY	YES	NO	ADDRESS	
PHONE		DIRECT	YES	NO		
EMAIL		SALARY			COMUTE TIME	
NOTES						

COMPANY		POSITION			APPLIED ON	
CONTACT		FOUND ON			LOCATION	
POSITION		AGENCY	YES	NO	ADDRESS	
PHONE		DIRECT	YES	NO		
EMAIL		SALARY			COMUTE TIME	
NOTES						

COMPANY		POSITION			APPLIED ON	
CONTACT		FOUND ON			LOCATION	
POSITION		AGENCY	YES	NO	ADDRESS	
PHONE		DIRECT	YES	NO		
EMAIL		SALARY			COMUTE TIME	
NOTES						

COMPANY		POSITION			APPLIED ON	
CONTACT		FOUND ON			LOCATION	
POSITION		AGENCY	YES	NO	ADDRESS	
PHONE		DIRECT	YES	NO		
EMAIL		SALARY			COMUTE TIME	
NOTES						

COMPANY		POSITION			APPLIFD ON	
CONTACT		FOUND ON			LOCATION	
POSITION		AGENCY	YES	NO	ADDRESS	
PHONE		DIRECT	YES	NO		
EMAIL		SALARY			COMUTE TIME	
NOTES						

NOTES

JOB APPLICATION TRACKER

COMPANY		POSITION		APPLIED ON	
CONTACT		FOUND ON		LOCATION	
POSITION		AGENCY	YES NO	ADDRESS	
PHONE		DIRECT	YES NO		
EMAIL		SALARY		COMUTE TIME	
NOTES					

COMPANY		POSITION		APPLIED ON	
CONTACT		FOUND ON		LOCATION	
POSITION		AGENCY	YES NO	ADDRESS	
PHONE		DIRECT	YES NO		
EMAIL		SALARY		COMUTE TIME	
NOTES					

COMPANY		POSITION		APPLIED ON	
CONTACT		FOUND ON		LOCATION	
POSITION		AGENCY	YES NO	ADDRESS	
PHONE		DIRECT	YES NO		
EMAIL		SALARY		COMUTE TIME	
NOTES					

COMPANY		POSITION		APPLIED ON	
CONTACT		FOUND ON		LOCATION	
POSITION		AGENCY	YES NO	ADDRESS	
PHONE		DIRECT	YES NO		
EMAIL		SALARY		COMUTE TIME	
NOTES					

COMPANY		POSITION		APPLIED ON	
CONTACT		FOUND ON		LOCATION	
POSITION		AGENCY	YES NO	ADDRESS	
PHONE		DIRECT	YES NO		
EMAIL		SALARY		COMUTE TIME	
NOTES					

NOTES

JOB APPLICATION TRACKER

COMPANY		POSITION		APPLIED ON	
CONTACT		FOUND ON		LOCATION	
POSITION		AGENCY	YES NO	ADDRESS	
PHONE		DIRECT	YES NO		
EMAIL		SALARY		COMUTE TIME	
NOTES					

COMPANY		POSITION		APPLIED ON	
CONTACT		FOUND ON		LOCATION	
POSITION		AGENCY	YES NO	ADDRESS	
PHONE		DIRECT	YES NO		
EMAIL		SALARY		COMUTE TIME	
NOTES					

COMPANY		POSITION		APPLIED ON	
CONTACT		FOUND ON		LOCATION	
POSITION		AGENCY	YES NO	ADDRESS	
PHONE		DIRECT	YES NO		
EMAIL		SALARY		COMUTE TIME	
NOTES					

COMPANY		POSITION		APPLIED ON	
CONTACT		FOUND ON		LOCATION	
POSITION		AGENCY	YES NO	ADDRESS	
PHONE		DIRECT	YES NO		
EMAIL		SALARY		COMUTE TIME	
NOTES					

COMPANY		POSITION		APPLIED ON	
CONTACT		FOUND ON		LOCATION	
POSITION		AGENCY	YES NO	ADDRESS	
PHONE		DIRECT	YES NO		
EMAIL		SALARY		COMUTE TIME	
NOTES					

NOTES

JOB APPLICATION TRACKER

COMPANY		POSITION		APPLIED ON	
CONTACT		FOUND ON		LOCATION	
POSITION		AGENCY	YES NO	ADDRESS	
PHONE		DIRECT	YES NO		
EMAIL		SALARY		COMUTE TIME	
NOTES					

COMPANY		POSITION		APPLIED ON	
CONTACT		FOUND ON		LOCATION	
POSITION		AGENCY	YES NO	ADDRESS	
PHONE		DIRECT	YES NO		
EMAIL		SALARY		COMUTE TIME	
NOTES					

COMPANY		POSITION		APPLIED ON	
CONTACT		FOUND ON		LOCATION	
POSITION		AGENCY	YES NO	ADDRESS	
PHONE		DIRECT	YES NO		
EMAIL		SALARY		COMUTE TIME	
NOTES					

COMPANY		POSITION		APPLIED ON	
CONTACT		FOUND ON		LOCATION	
POSITION		AGENCY	YES NO	ADDRESS	
PHONE		DIRECT	YES NO		
EMAIL		SALARY		COMUTE TIME	
NOTES					

COMPANY		POSITION		APPLIED ON	
CONTACT		FOUND ON		LOCATION	
POSITION		AGENCY	YES NO	ADDRESS	
PHONE		DIRECT	YES NO		
EMAIL		SALARY		COMUTE TIME	
NOTES					

NOTES